THE LITTLE
BOOK OF

SHIT
JOKES

THE LITTLE BOOK OF SHIT JOKES

An Hachette UK Company
www.hachette.co.uk

Summersdale Publishers Ltd
Part of Octopus Publishing Group Limited
Carmelite House
50 Victoria Embankment
LONDON
EC4Y 0DZ
UK

www.summersdale.com

Printed and bound in China

ISBN: 978-1-78783-028-8

Substantial discounts on bulk quantities of Summersdale books are available to corporations, professional associations and other organizations. For details contact general enquiries: telephone: +44 (0) 1243 771107 or email: enquiries@summersdale.com.

THE LITTLE BOOK OF 👎

SHIT JOKES

Sid Finch

summersdale

My dog used to love chasing people on a bike.

It got so bad I had to take his bike away.

Why did the inventor scrap his belt made of watches?

It was a waist of time.

I called my boss and whispered I wouldn't be in as I had a wee cough.

He seemed surprised. "You have a wee cough?!"

"Thanks!" I said. "See you Monday!"

What do you call a snowman in the Bahamas?

A puddle.

"What's your favourite thing about Switzerland?"

"Well, the flag is a big plus."

Somebody stole my luggage, leaving only the handle, lock and wheels. I took it to the local police station and laid the parts in front of an officer.

He said I didn't have much of a case.

I love when the Earth
fully rotates.

It really makes my day.

My dad is always telling
me I should go and
live my dreams.

Thing is, I don't want
to be naked in an exam
I forgot to study for.

What do you call cheese that isn't yours?

Nacho cheese.

Believe it or not, astronauts can have parties in space.

They just have to planet.

A gang of jump leads walk into a bar.

The barman says, "I'll serve you, but don't start anything."

"Doctor, doctor, I keep dreaming that I'm drowning in an ocean of fizzy orange liquid!"

"Don't worry. It's just a Fanta sea."

A lot of people cry when they cut an onion.

The trick is not to get too attached.

A dad took his two sons to the zoo. They walked around dozens of empty enclosures, disappointed, before finally arriving at the one pen to contain anything at all: a single dog.

The dad turned to his sons and said, "Well, kids – this is a Shih Tzu."

Two slabs of tarmac have a bad reputation around their local bar. One day, even they fall silent as a slab of red tarmac enters.

"Watch out for him," one of them says. "He's a bit of a cycle path."

I was going to tell you a brilliant joke about time travel.

Unfortunately, you didn't like it.

My wife always says,
"Cheer up. You could
be trapped in a vertical
water-filled tunnel."

I know she means well.

I shaved my head last
week and finally bought
myself a cheap wig.

It was a small-price toupee.

A policeman stopped a woman driving a car full of monkeys. "What on earth are you doing?" he said. "Here's £100 – take them straight to the zoo!" Later that evening, as the policeman was clocking off, he stopped the same woman with the same monkeys in her car.

"Hey! I gave you £100 to take these monkeys to the zoo!" he said.

"I know," replied the woman. "But we had some money left over, so I took them for ice cream after."

I could only ever recognize 25 letters of the alphabet.

I don't know why.

I forgot which way I threw my boomerang.

But then it came back to me.

**My dad thought
he had 97 cows.**

**But when he rounded
them up he had 100.**

**Why are actors told
to break a leg?**

**Because every play
has to have a cast.**

**My friend's wedding
was so emotional.**

Even the cake was in tiers.

**What do you get if you cross
a dog with a magician?**

A labra-cadabra-dor.

I went to my uncle's house for dinner.

"How many burgers would you like?" he asked.

"Just one," I replied.

"Now, there's no need to be polite," said my uncle.

"Oh, OK. Just one, you smelly idiot."

Why was Cinderella terrible at sports?

Because her coach was a pumpkin.

What do you eat when you're cold and angry?

A brr-grr.

Did you hear about the woman who invented the door knocker?

She won the "no-bell" prize.

Two drums and a cymbal fall off a cliff.

Ba-dum, tisch!

I gave away my vacuum cleaner the other day.

It was only collecting dust.

I bought two litres of correction fluid yesterday.

Huge mistake.

I thought I'd gain an advantage in the snail race by removing my racer's shell, but if anything it made him more sluggish.

What do you get when you tell a joke that's secretly a rhetorical question?

What has four legs but can't walk?

Two pairs of trousers.

My girlfriend is on a tropical-food diet – she's filled the entire house with fruit.

It's enough to make a mango crazy.

At first I refused to believe my mother was stealing from the motorway.

But when I got home all the signs were there.

Why did the chicken cross the road?

Beats me. But he looked like he was up to something fowl.

My aunt has never
smoked a day in her life.

She normally gets
tired around dusk.

The caretaker at my work
climbed to the top of
a big tree outside and
invited me to join him.

I refused. I don't get on with
high-maintenance people.

**Generally I
enjoy mathematics.**

**But graphs are where
I draw the line.**

**A girl came up to me and
said she recognized me
from her vegetarian group.**

**Which is strange, because
I'd never seen herbivore.**

A man walks into a bar with a newt on his shoulder.

The barman says, "We don't get a lot of those in here. What's his name?"

"Tiny," says the man.

"Why tiny?"

"Because he's my-newt."

My husband has a compulsion to line up crockery in the most unusual way.

It's a rare dish order.

I invented a speed-dating business for the final chapters of books, but gave it up after a month.

I couldn't make ends meet.

**What do you call a
three-footed aardvark?**

A yard-vark.

**What are the two strongest
days of the week?**

**Saturday and Sunday.
The others are all weekdays.**

At half-time, a coach sat next to his striker and put a hand on his shoulder.

"What made you come and try out for us today?" he asked.

The striker said, "Ever since I was a kid, I wanted to play football so badly."

The coach replied, "Well, you're succeeding."

Teacher: What's the difference between lightning and electricity?

Pupil: The lightning bill doesn't make my dad swear.

My dad is always yelling, "Did you hear what I just said?!"

Honestly, who starts a conversation like that?

Why does Tiger Woods always bring extra socks to golf tournaments?

In case he gets a hole-in-one.

Albert Einstein eventually devised a whole theory of space.

It was about time, too!

A woman was circling a park, bouncing her
bawling baby on her hip and saying,
"It's OK, Emma. It'll be OK. Calm down,
Emma. Everything is fine."

An elderly lady complimented the woman on
how well she was soothing little Emma.

The woman replied, "My baby's
called Jade. I'm Emma."

As a doctor, I've never made a joke about an unvaccinated hippopotamus.

But I'll give anything a shot.

Why did the coffee call the police?

Because it got mugged.

How did the hipster burn her mouth?

She drank her coffee before it was cool.

People are always really impressed with my homemade ice cream.

I got the recipe at sundae school.

Did you hear about the four men who stole a calendar?

They each got three months.

"Doctor, doctor, it took me a year to notice I'm a football!"

"You must want to kick yourself."

Two young boys were talking in a playground. "My dad was on TV last night," the first boy said. "He's a politician."

"Honest?" said his friend.

"No," replied the first boy. "Just the regular kind."

Why did the ghost with unfinished business cross the road?

To get to the other side.

I bought the world's worst thesaurus last week.

It's was really, really, really not good at all.

I've been trying to buy some camouflage trousers for my friend, but I can't find any.

Why do fish swim
in salt water?

Because swimming in
pepper water would
make them sneeze.

A teacher asks her class, "What is the name of the tallest type of building?"

One boy raises his hand. "Libraries," he says.

The teacher looks puzzled. "Why do you say that?"

The boy replies, "Because they have the most stories."

I saw an advert for a broken radio: "Bargain price, volume stuck on high."

I thought, "I can't turn that down."

What did one wall say to the other wall?

"Meet me in the corner!"

Did you hear about the bed that ended up with a compulsively tidy owner?

It was made for life.

Why are ghosts such bad liars?

You can see right through them.

A girl in California spent $200 to hire a limousine to take her to her prom. When she got outside, the car was sitting there empty, with a note to say the driver was not included.

Her father came out and found her looking upset. "What's wrong, sweetie?" he asked.

The girl gestured at the limo. "I spent all that money and I have nothing to chauffeur it."

Did you hear about the actor who fell through the floorboards?

It was just a stage she was going through.

I've got an irrational fear of negative numbers.

I'll stop at nothing to avoid them.

Give a man a fish and you feed him for a day.

But teach a man to fish and you get rid of him for whole weekends at a time.

"Doctor, doctor, I'm worried about my eyesight."

"You should be – this is a garden centre."

A peninsula and a small island are discussing holidaymakers.

"They'll love you," says the island. "You're so interesting."

"How do you know?" says the peninsula.

The island replies, "Just trust me. I'm a hundred per cent shore."

Billy was late for school. When his
teacher asked him why, he told her
he was dreaming about a football match.

His teacher looked confused and said,
"But that doesn't explain why you're late."

Billy replied, "It went to penalties."

What's the fastest liquid on Earth?

Milk – it's pasteurized before you know it.

I read in a book: "Don't dress for the job you have; dress for the job you want."

It's easy to say, but when I turned up in my lifeguard shorts the other undertakers were not impressed.

I was supposed to meet my date at the gym, but they never showed up.

Looks like we aren't going to work out.

Why did the criminal steal a hand-blender?

It was a whisk he was willing to take.

A giraffe walks into a bar
and orders a pint of beer
and a packet of nuts.

"That'll be nine-fifty," says the
barman. He cleans a few glasses
and then adds, "We don't get
a lot of giraffes in here."

The giraffe says, "At those prices,
I'm surprised you get anyone."

How did the mathematician clear his ears of wax?

He worked it out with a pencil.

What goes down but doesn't come up?

A yo.

**My mother asked me
to bring her something
hard to write on.**

**I don't know why she got
so mad. *I* think marbles
are very hard to write on.**

**It's easy to stop women from
drinking fabric softener, but
it's harder to deter gents.**

A woman in a restaurant spots another woman enjoying a steak. She calls the waiter over, points and says, "I'll have what she's having."

Two minutes later the waiter returns with sauce up his sleeves and half a plate of food. "It was a bit of a struggle," he said. "But I got it."

**What hangs from the ceiling
and looks like a lampshade?**

A hippo in disguise.

**What do you call a
big heap of cats?**

A meow-ntain.

"Grandma, can I go to the toilet?"

"Jenny, *may* I go to the toilet?"

"I asked first!"

Why did Humpty Dumpty have a great fall?

To get over his disappointing summer.

Pupil: I didn't bring my calculator today...

Teacher: ... and?

Pupil: ... I've got nothing to add.

What do you call a dinosaur that looks after its teeth?

A flossiraptor.

A man sits on a bench beside a woman and a dog. The man asks the woman, "Does your dog bite?"

"Certainly not!" the woman replies.

The man reaches down to pet the dog and the dog bites him. "I thought you said your dog doesn't bite!" the man exclaims.

"She doesn't," the woman replies. "That isn't my dog."

Do you know Murphy's Law? It says that anything that can go wrong will go wrong. But have you heard of Cole's law?

It's thinly sliced cabbage.

Teacher: Can someone tell me the plural of sheep?

Pupil: ... sheep?

Teacher: Correct! And the plural of baby?

Pupil: ... twins?

The dictionary I bought today is just a book of blank pages.

I have no words to describe how upset I am.

What is green, fuzzy, has four legs and would kill you if it jumped on you?

A snooker table.

A piece of string walks into a bar.

"Hey!" says the barman. "We don't serve string in here!"

The piece of string leaves, ties a tight bow in himself and rolls on the ground. When he goes back into the bar, the barman says, "Aren't you that piece of string I slung out?"

The string replies, "No, I'm a frayed knot."

My girlfriend left me
because I'm too insecure.

No, wait, she's back.
She just went to turn
the heating off.

Which word has five letters,
but becomes shorter when
you add two more?

Short.

When does a joke become a dad joke?

When it becomes apparent.

"Doctor, doctor, I keep referring to people as days of the week."

"Take two of these and call me Monday."

Having lost her job, a woman packs her things and leaves the building. On the way out, a security guard touches her lightly on the shoulder. "Hey," he says warmly. "Plethora."

"Thanks," says the woman. "That means a lot."

Today, I shocked the postman by opening the door in a horror mask.

I don't know what surprised him most: the mask, or the fact I know where he lives.

Patient: I'm sorry, doctor – I'm just so nervous. This is my first operation.

Doctor: That's OK. It's mine too!

How do you stop a dog from barking in the morning?

Take away its alarm clock.

A limbo dancer walks into a bar.

She's immediately disqualified.

What washes up on really small beaches?

Micro-waves.

What happened when the magician got frustrated?

He pulled his hare out.

A man walked into a fishmonger's with a mackerel on his shoulder.

"Do you make fishcakes?" the man asked.

"We sure do," said the fishmonger.

"Great," said the man. "
"It's his birthday."

What do you get if you divide the circumference of a pumpkin by its diameter?

Pumpkin pi.

Did you hear about the explosion at the French cheese factory?

There was nothing left but de brie.

I quit my job as PA to a helium addict.

I refuse to be spoken to in that tone of voice.

What does ET stand for?

The national anthem.

A man at the bank asked me to help check his balance.

It wasn't great – when I pushed him he went right over.

I walked into a bookshop
and asked if they had a
section on paranoia.

The attendant said,
"It's right behind you!"

What did the cannibal
get when he arrived
late for dinner?

The cold shoulder.

My poet friend isn't very good at his craft. The other day he said, "What rhymes with purple."

I replied, "No it doesn't."

A clown pulled my chair out for me at dinner.

I thought it was a nice jester.

A man walks into a bar with a crocodile under one arm and a chicken under the other.

"I'll have a beer," says the man.

"And a cider for me," says the crocodile.

"Wow," says the barman.
"Is that a talking crocodile?"

"No," says the man. "The chicken's a ventriloquist."

I just published a book
on reverse psychology.

I'd advise that you
definitely don't buy it.

What do you call a
bear with no ears?

A B.

My husband demanded that I stop acting like a flamingo.

I really had to put my foot down.

A book just fell on my head.

I only have my shelf to blame.

My friend has started heckling desserts.

Personally, I don't like to boo meringue. It always comes back to get you.

When geese fly together, do you know why one side of the "V" is longer than the other?

Because it has more geese in it.

Manager: Our new signing cost thirty million. I call him our "wonder player".

Interviewer: Is he that good?

Manager: No. But whenever I see him play, I wonder why I bought him.

What did the octogenarian pirate say?

Aye, matey!

Did you hear the one about the broken pencil?

Never mind. It's pointless.

The other day my girlfriend asked me to pass her lipstick, but I accidentally gave her a glue stick instead.

She still isn't talking to me.

My bike won't stop attacking people on my journey to work.

It's a vicious cycle.

A man is standing in front of the mirror. He says to his wife, "There's fat bunching around my hips. I've got tufts of hair in my ears, and since we've been married my muscles have all but gone. And I think I might be going bald."

Without looking up, his wife replies, "At least there's nothing wrong with your eyes."

I really wanted to find out the lowest ranking position in the army.

But people kept telling me it was private.

I'd just like to shout out to all my friends who don't know the opposite of "in".

For Christmas, I bought my kids luminescent dental braces.

I can't wait to see their little faces light up.

The sultanas down the road are having a bake-sale this week.

I'm just raisin awareness.

At church, a little girl tells her mother she's going to be sick. Her mother tells her to do it in the bushes. The girl leaves and comes back after about five minutes. Her mother asks her if she threw up. "Yes," the girl says. "But I didn't have to go round the back – there was a little box by the front door that said: 'For the Sick'."

**My therapist tells me I have
an unhealthy obsession
with vengeance.**

We'll see about that.

**I had to quit my job defusing
bombs on the sea floor.**

**I couldn't handle
the pressure.**

What did the drummer name his twin daughters?

Anna1, Anna2...

I get all nostalgic when I reverse my car.

It really takes me back.

What's the best time to go to the dentist?

2.30.

What type of cheese surrounds a medieval castle?

Moatzerella.

**Teacher: Repeat after me:
I run through the campsite.**

**Pupil: Miss, isn't it "I *ran*
through the campsite?"**

**Teacher: Why do
you say that?**

**Pupil: Because it's
past tents.**

My boyfriend borrowed £300 when I first met him. When we broke up four years later, he returned my £300 exactly.

I lost interest in that relationship.

I know vegans think people who sell meat are gross.

But people who sell fruit and vegetables are grocer.

What's the difference between bird flu and swine flu?

Bird flu requires tweetment, whereas swine flu just needs a little oinkment.

I'm struggling to meet my deadline so I tattooed a clock on my hip.

Anything to keep time on my side.

Two cricket teammates were having a pint. One said to the other, "You're looking glum."

The other replied, "I am. My doctor told me I can't play cricket."

His friend took a sip of his drink. "I could have told you that."

Daughter: Dad! How long will you be in the bath?

Dad: Still six foot two.

What has a funny smell and flies?

Mouldy cheese.

My doctor told me I was losing my hearing.

I think I'm fine, though. I mean, I haven't heard anything since.

My grandma bet me I couldn't build a motorbike out of spaghetti.

You should have seen her face when I drove pasta.

A woman enters a circus tent and asks for a job.

"Well," says the circus manager. "What can you do?"

"I can do a great impression of a bird," she replies.

"Pfft," says the circus manager. "So can lots of people."

"Oh well," says the woman, and she flies away.

If you're interested in finding out more about our books, find us on Facebook at **Summersdale Publishers** and follow us on Twitter at **@Summersdale**.

www.summersdale.com